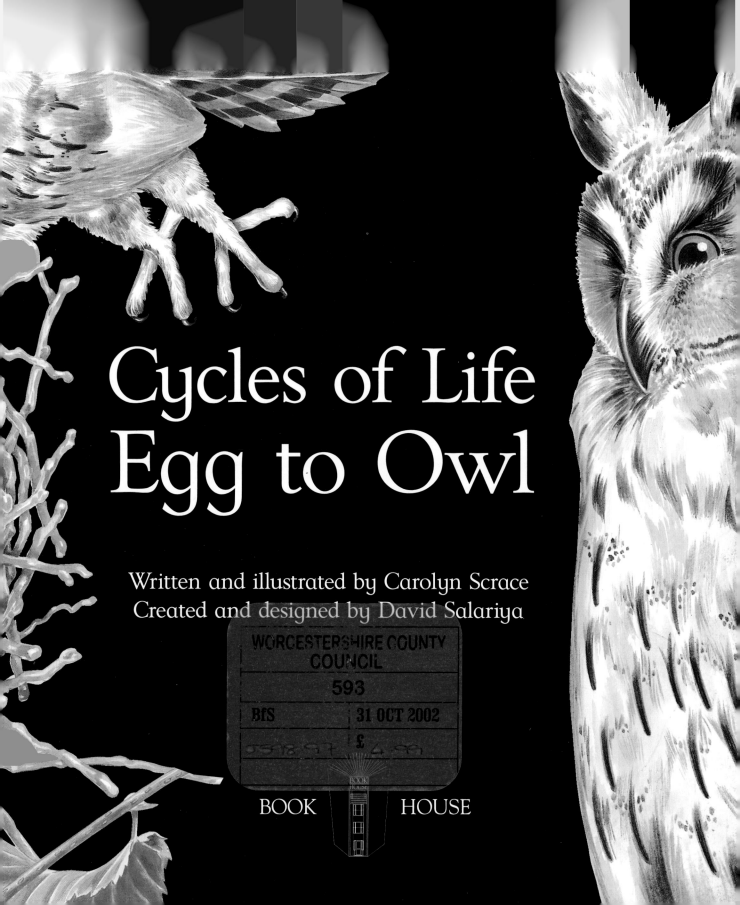

# Cycles of Life
# Egg to Owl

Written and illustrated by Carolyn Scrace
Created and designed by David Salariya

BOOK          HOUSE

# Contents

# Introduction

Birds have two wings and are covered in feathers. Most birds, like the long-eared owl, can fly.

A long-eared owl begins its life inside an egg. When it has grown big enough, the baby owl breaks its way out of the eggshell.

In this book you can see the amazing cycle of life of a long-eared owl, from egg to owl.

# Mating

The male owl chooses a place to build a nest.

He then finds a female owl by flying and calling in a special way.

When the female sees him she calls back.

The male and female owl then mate.

A long-eared owl has large orange eyes and long ear tufts. These are not its ears.

Ear tuft

Female

Butterfly

Nest

8

Elm tree

# Building a nest

Long-eared owls
usually nest in the
old nests of other birds
like crows, magpies,
ravens or herons.

The owls line their
nest with moss,
leaves, feathers and
small pieces of bark.

The nest is high up in
the tree and is hidden
amongst the branches.

11

# Laying eggs

The female owl lays
from three to five eggs.
The eggs are white
and an oval shape.

The female sits on
her eggs to keep them
safe and warm.
Inside the eggs,
the tiny owls grow.

Sometimes the male owl
sits on the eggs while the
female hunts for food.

Egg

Caterpillar

12

Nestling

# The eggs hatch

After four weeks,
the first egg starts
to hatch. The tiny
owl cracks open
the eggshell.

When the baby owl
comes out of the egg
it is called a nestling.
Nestlings are covered
in fluffy, white
feathers called down.

15

# Hunting

At night, the male owl
flies off and catches
food for the nestlings.

The male owl takes
food back to the nest.
The female owl gives
little bits to each baby.

Long-eared owls
hunt at night and
find their prey in
total darkness.

Butterfly chrysalis

# Feeding

Long-eared owls eat voles, mice, rats and other rodents, small rabbits and sometimes birds or snakes.

The older nestlings make a call that sounds like a squeaky gate.

19

# Exploring

Three weeks after hatching, the young owls can leave the nest.

They use their beaks and wings to climb and jump along the branches close to the nest.

Other birds and animals like to eat long-eared owls. The adult owls keep watch over the young owls.

Butterfly hatching

# Cat attack!

When a cat comes near the nest, the female owl makes herself look as big and scary as she can.

She puffs out her feathers, spreads her wings out like a fan and stares at the cat with her huge orange eyes.

The adult owls make a barking sound to frighten away the cat.

23

# Learning to fly

Five weeks after hatching, the young owls begin to fly. At first they only fly a short distance.

They are always hungry and each night call for their parents to feed them.

A young owl is very curious. To help it see in every direction, the young owl can turn its head almost completely round in a circle!

# Leaving the nest

Two months after hatching, the young owls can hunt for their own food.

It is time for them to fly away and leave the nest.

Long-eared owls usually live alone and only come together to mate and raise a family.

# The cycle of egg to owl

In spring, a pair of long-eared owls build a nest. The female lays about three to five eggs.

About four weeks later, the eggs begin to hatch. The baby owls are called nestlings and are covered in white down.

During the next few weeks, the nestlings remain in the nest. They eat lots and grow bigger and stronger.

28

About three weeks after hatching the young owls are able to leave the nest and explore their surroundings.

Two weeks later (five weeks after hatching) they begin learning how to fly. Their parents still feed them.

When they are about two months old, the young owls leave the nest and hunt for their own food.

# Egg to owl words

**Beak**
The hard and pointed area around the mouth of a bird.

**Bird**
An animal that has two wings and is covered in feathers. Most birds can fly.

**Down**
Soft, white and fluffy feathers.

**Ear tufts**
Long feathery tufts on the top of the owl's head. These are not actually the owl's ears.

**Egg**
A container that holds the tiny, baby bird.

**Feathers**
The light and soft covering of birds.

**Hatching**
When the baby bird leaves its egg.

**Mating**
When a male and female join together to raise a family.

**Mouse**
A small rodent.

**Nest**
A cup shape made of sticks. Used by a bird as a home for its young.

**Nestling**
A bird that is too young to leave the nest.

**Prey**
The animal that another animal catches to eat.

**Rodent**
An animal with two long, curved teeth which it uses for gnawing.

**Shell**
The thin hard covering of an egg. It keeps the baby bird safe as it grows.

**Vole**
A small rodent, similar to a mouse.

# Index

Language Consultant:
Betty Root

Editors:
Karen Barker Smith
Stephanie Cole

Natural History Consultant:
Dr Gerald Legg

Published in Great Britain in 2002 by
Book House, an imprint of
**The Salariya Book Company Ltd**
Book House, 25 Marlborough Place,
Brighton BN1 1UB

Visit the Salariya Book Company at:
**www.salariya.com**
**www.book-house.co.uk**

A catalogue record for this book is
available from the British Library.

ISBN  1 904194 25 7
Printed and bound in China.

Printed on paper from
sustainable forests.